# Positive Tl

## _The Most Efficient Guide on Positive Thinking, Overcoming Negativity and Finding Success & Happiness_

# Jack Morris

# Contents

# **<u>Introduction</u>**

I want to thank you and congratulate you for downloading the book, "Positive Thinking: The Most Efficient Guide on Positive Thinking, Overcoming Negativity and Finding Success & Happiness".

This book contains proven steps and strategies on how to change your mindset and attitude, and become a more positive person. Through this book, you will learn about the powers of positive thinking and negative thinking, and how you should use both to your benefit.

This book also contains useful information regarding the practices that successful people have. It is through this book that you will learn about the techniques that you have to do in order for you to live a happier, healthier, and more successful life.

It also features 10 great easy to follow habits that successful, positive people use in their day-to-day lives, and how you can implement them to your own.

Is your glass half full or half empty? Is the grass greener on the other side? Your outlook on these lifelong rhetorical questions could determine the path on which you chase life on, and could even play a role in your general health and well-being.

There was a popular speaker who started off a seminar once by holding up a $20 bill. A crowd of 200 had gathered to hear him speak. He asked the crowd, "Who would like this $20 bill?"

200 hands went up.

He said, "I am going to give this $20 to one of you but first, let me do this." He crumpled the bill up.

He then asked, "Who still wants it?"

All 200 hands were still raised.

"Well," he replied, "What if I do this?" Then he dropped the bill on the ground and stomped on it with his shoes.

He picked it up, and showed it to the crowd. The bill was all crumpled and dirty.

"Now who still wants it?"

All the hands still went up.

"My friends, I have just shown you a very important lesson. No matter what I did to the money, you still wanted it because it did not decrease in value. It was still worth $20. Many times in our lives, life crumples us and grinds us into the dirt. We make bad decisions or deal with poor circumstances. We feel worthless. But no matter what has happened or what will happen, you will never lose your value. You are special – Don't ever forget it!"

Many obstacles will present themselves throughout our lives, and it is in each and every one of us to tackle them in our own way. Approaching theses obstacles with a positive attitude will not only ease your journey, but it will build you into thinking positively consistently, therefor creating a healthier mentality and general way of life. Positive things come from positive thoughts.

To prove how little, you have to do to start thinking positively I'd ask you, wherever you're reading this, be it a train, bus, lunch hour or at home, I want you to smile to the next person you see, without rhyme or reason, just smile. A smile is the most contagious expression we can use, and is almost always reciprocated. It is a gift where we can gain just as much as we give, and releases endorphins making us feel more positive instantly. Introducing little acts of positivity is an effective way in becoming more consistent with having a more optimistic outlook on life, and will soon become a permanent part of you.

Thanks again for downloading this book, I hope you enjoy it!

# Chapter 1:

# The Power of Positive Thinking

Positive thinking is a concept that people say all the time. Mental health professionals as well as gurus often advise others to stay positive, even when they find themselves embroiled in difficult situations. It is actually easy to say to stay positive, but it can be quite difficult to do. During times of chaos, famine, calamities, and problems, it can be very hard to look for the good side.

Nonetheless, having a positive mental attitude that prompts you to expect favorable results is crucial. It allows you to be healthier, happier, and more productive. Even if your level of optimism is not that high, it can still help you attain your goals and objectives.

Positive thinking is a process that you have to learn and adopt into your day-to-day life. When you maintain a positive mindset, you become empowered to increase your levels of satisfaction and happiness. What's more, positive thinking can help you become successful. You can try asking successful people. They are most likely going to tell you that they, too, have experienced adversities that made them almost quit. But they didn't; because they have a positive mindset.

Successful, productive, and effective people have a positive attitude. They know what they want. They are focused. They do not let downtimes get the best of them. You have to realize that everybody experiences adversities because nobody is perfect. All people have problems. You may just not notice other people having a hard time because they have a healthy attitude towards their situation. If you become an optimistic individual, you will already be many steps ahead of your peers. The secret to staying positive is taking full control of your thoughts.

Keep in mind that success is ninety percent the direct result of the way you use your mind. The best athletes, businessmen, and professionals know the importance of using their mind properly. Henry Ford, founder of the well-known Ford Motor Company, said that you are right whether you think you can or cannot do something.

Oftentimes, people fail before they even start an undertaking. This happens because they do not use their minds properly. They use imaginary fears, negative feelings, and past failures to scare themselves away from going after their dreams and goals in life.

You have to take note that there isn't really a prerequisite for your success. You just have to believe in your own abilities.

You have to exert effort in convincing yourself that you have the capability to succeed in life.

You cannot convince yourself that you can merely trust your skills once or twice and then make an actually difference in your life. You have to be persistent and faithful in your own abilities. You have to truly believe that you can do it. You can practice by telling yourself positive affirmations every day. Then, you can progress to doing it every week, every month, and so on.

Once you develop this habit, it would be difficult for you to stop. Once you reach a point where you are already confident in your own skills, the energies in your body will give you a rush.

Your mind creates your world. That is a fact. You can prove this by looking around you. Think of all the things you see, from the lighting fixtures to the furniture pieces in your home. Look outside your window and watch the birds and butterfly fly. Admire the plants and trees, and the wonders of nature. Remember that whatever your mind conceives, it is able to create.

If you are thinking that positive thinking strategies are shady, you should try holding off on forming snap judgments until you try using positive thinking for your life choices. You may be surprised with what you discover.

## Positive Thinking and Quantum Physics

Positive thinking and quantum physics are actually interconnected. Even the greatest philosophers of all time, such as Jesus and the Buddha, have practiced the power of the mind. Quantum physics is actually the cause of curiosity for the Universe as well as the desire to learn how it works scientifically.

Researchers of quantum physics continually discover that your beliefs and perceptions on reality can alert such reality to fit a particular perspective. Many scientists have already done experiments in their hopes of discovering that the Universe's basic building blocks are either waves or particles. They kept arguing with regard to the results of the experiments. Eventually, they started using new ways for their experiments.

The scientists learned that these basic building blocks turned into particles or waves, but only depending on what the scientists expected them to be. For instance, when the scientists wanted them to turn into particles, they turned into particles. When the scientists wanted them to turn into waves, they turned into waves.

You can apply the same principle into your own life. Whatever you believe is your reality is actually going to be your reality. It happens that way because it is what you expected to happen. This is the very reason why a lot of successful people consider their minds as their most important asset. They are aware of the fact that their beliefs create their realities.

## Causes of Positive Thinking

When you harbor positive thoughts in your mind, your body releases positive energy. This is good for both your mental and physical health.

Through positive thinking, you can alleviate stress and tension. More often than not, people get too engrossed in their work that they forget to relax. Their hectic schedules prevent them from taking time to rest and have fun. They are consumed by the problems they have at work, and they tend to bring these problems home.

This kind of behavior is what affects their lives in a negative manner. If you see yourself in these people, you have to change your mindset and habits immediately. Otherwise, you will find yourself in much worse situations. Worrying nonstop is never good. Stress is actually detrimental to health and can increase risks of heart diseases, cancers, high blood pressure, and diabetes among other illnesses.

If you are stressed out all the time, various aspects of your life can get affected. It can also make you frustrated and cause you to release your frustration to other people. If you do this frequently, your personal and professional relationships can get strained. It is not advisable to take out your negative feelings on others. You may end up alone and gain a negative reputation.

On the other hand, if you practice positive thinking, you will develop good habits on how to deal with stressful situations. In spite of chaos and adversity, you will stay calm and rational. You will also see the positive side of the situation, no matter how negative it seems. Because of this, you will be able to come up with reasonable and sound decisions.

It is actually how you perceive things that predict the outcome of your life. You can even reduce your risk of mental health problems such as depression and anxiety if you change the way you look at everything.

According to a study published in the Journal of American College Health, using positive affirmations and other cognitive behavioral techniques can reduce negative thinking patterns as well as symptoms of depression. In a similar study done by researchers at the University of Kentucky, Lexington, it was found that positive thinking and habits can benefit your overall health.

Moreover, positive thinking can boost your confidence levels and improve your relationships. In spite of your shortcomings, you will still be confident enough to do the things that you want. You will find ways on how to turn your weaknesses into strengths.

# Chapter 2:

# The Power of Negative Thinking

Various work cultures are involved in various issues. In bureaucracies, for instance, people have a hard time accepting new ideologies. They are most likely to turn down new ideas and propositions because they think that they will not work. In startups, however, ideas are regarded either as disruptive or great. Teams are often encouraged to remain positive and accept every new idea. The same concept happens in other aspects of life.

If you yearn to have emotional freedom, you have to understand that whatever problems you believe you have at the moment are not actual problems. Your real problem is that you are not aware of how you have to think correctly about your problems.

Your experiences are meant to teach you new ways of thinking. If you do not learn how to have a different point of view, you get stuck in your old ways. Instead of moving forward, you become stagnant.

You see, the more you experience things, the better you become at viewing the world with a new set of lenses. You start to think with better dimensions and consider the possibilities that you previously did not believe in.

As you go on with life, you learn how to ignore your negative thoughts by disassociating with them. Your negative thoughts actually give you as much information as your positive thoughts. So, instead of feeling fear towards them, you should view them as your directives.

This is where the power of negative thinking lies. You can be like the stoics who practiced negative thinking and visualization to prepare for the worst-case scenarios. You learn how to think when you recognize how to apply emotion and meaning into your life. If you do not make decisions on a conscious level, you will continue following feeling patterns and responding to situations the way you did when you were younger.

To solve your problems, you do not necessarily have to overly focus on the positive, but rather learn how you can convert the dark sides of your mind to something that can encourage you to grow and make good changes in your life. You attain inner peace and emotional freedom when you become aware of what you have to do during the times negative feelings and thoughts start to arise.

You regulate your emotions when you think of them. Your prefrontal cortex allows you to think of your own mind. Your brain thinks of itself. This is what psychologists refer to as metacognition.

This explains why you know when you are angry. Every feeling you have comes with a sense of self-awareness. Hence, you are able to figure out the reason why you feel that way. If you do not have self-awareness, you cannot know if you are afraid of something. This would prevent you to take the appropriate course of action, such as running away or escaping.

More importantly, if your feeling does not make sense to you or if your amygdala responds to loss frame, you can simply ignore it. Your prefrontal cortex may select to ignore your emotional brain once it notices that giving meaning to it will not make any sense.

So, when you think that you have a problem, you do not really have one. It is actually the way you see the issue that becomes the problem. You tend to view it as a problem instead of viewing it as a signal that your brain does not want to respond to. You view the situation as a problem instead of a fallacy in your own understanding, perception, and focus.

In order for you to function normally, you must learn how to deal with your emotions. You see, discernment is what differentiates debilitating anxiety from the fear that enables you to take courageous actions. Discernment also requires practice. You have to do it over and over until it becomes a habit. Also, awareness and knowledge enable people to convert obstacles to opportunities so that they will not be crushed by their uncertainties.

When you become uncomfortable, you become forced to think of possibilities that you have not thought of before. This is the reason heartbreak is vital for growth. The struggles and sufferings you experience enable you to learn about appreciation, understanding, and sensitivity. Any person can see and enjoy the positivity in their lives. However, it is only the truly intelligent ones who can take the negativity and see something more profound in it.

## The Effects of Negative Thinking

In 2012, over twenty individuals were treated for burns in a hospital in San Jose, California. They participated in an event hosted by Tony Robbins, a well-known motivational speaker, and walked over burning coals while barefoot.

You may have heard of people successfully walking over coals while barefoot. This may have happened because coal is not a good conductor for heat. So, a person can successfully walk over it without getting harmed.

In the event, however, the participants were told that everything is a matter of the mind. They were told that they can succeed if they believe they could. In the end, they got burned.

While positive thinking can surely be beneficial, you have to realize that good can also come out of the negative. Thus, you should not try too hard to focus on positivity. You should also reconsider your relationship with negative situations and emotions.

Gabriele Oettingen, a psychologist, along with her colleagues did a research on positive thinking. They found that positive visualization could make individuals less likely to get what they aim for under some conditions. The participants of the study were deprived of water and they became dehydrated for a while. One group was asked to visualize water while the rest were asked to have neutral or negative visualizations. The researchers found that those who visualized water experienced a reduction in their energy levels.

In a similar study done at the University of Waterloo, the researchers found that using positive affirmations such as cheery slogans to lift the mood of people could actually make them feel worse, especially if they suffer from low self-esteem. They feel worse because reciting the positive affirmations only make them think of themselves as unlovable or unlikable.

In business settings, aiming for a specific goal can be detrimental to the company. When employees become fixated on achieving a particular objective, they begin to lose track of the mission of their organization. They may even reach the point where they sacrifice ethics for financial or career success.

Ancient spiritual gurus and philosophers have long known that positivity and negativity have to be balanced. You need to be optimistic and pessimistic at the same time. You have to strive for security and success while also being prepared for uncertainty and failure.

In fact, the Stoics suggest that you visualize the worst thing that can possibly happen so that you can reduce your anxiety towards the future. If you can see how bad your future can be, you would be able to cope. They also said that when you know you can lose your possessions and relationships, you become more grateful for them. For them, positive thinking makes you lean into your future and ignore your present happiness.

Similarly, Buddhist meditation encourages you to let your sensations and emotions come and go, without forcing yourself to think positive thoughts. According to an article published in The Journal of Pain in 2009, becoming non-judgmental towards pain rather than refusing to feel it can significantly reduce it.

Through these perspectives, you will realize that positive thinking can make you more stressed out trying to get rid of traces of negativity instead of feeling joyful. If you tell yourself that everything is going to work out, you will not be able to prepare yourself in case it does not.

# Chapter 3:

# How to Overcome Negative Thoughts

Negative thoughts can drag you down. They make you feel sorry for yourself and discourage you from taking action. They make you walk around with a rain cloud over your head. If you continue to harbor negative thoughts, you will hold yourself back and prevent yourself from living life the way you want to.

The best way to overcome your negative thoughts is make an effort to change the way you think. When you change your mindset, you will be able to change your behavior. The following tips are effective in helping people overcome their negative thoughts:

**Find what is helpful or good when you find yourself in a seemingly negative situation.**

Everybody experiences setbacks and failures. When you do not get what you want, you may feel negative emotions and cause you to see things in a negative manner. When this happens, you have to counter it by asking certain questions. These questions should help you feel better as well as help you grow.

For example, you can ask yourself what good thing you can see in the situation or what you can do differently in case you find yourself in the same situation in the future. What should you do so that you can get better results? You can also ask yourself about the lesson that you have learned from the experience. Furthermore, you can put yourself in the shoes of other people. What do you think your friends will tell you or advise you to do to effectively deal with the situation you are in.

**Remind yourself that other people do not really care about what you do or say.**

You may harbor negative thoughts when you start thinking that other people may think or say something about you. This causes you to over analyze things to the point of no longer being rational. If you continue to do this, you will soon lose touch of reality and get caught up in your negative thoughts.

You have to realize that people do not really have a lot of energy or time to talk about you or think about the things you do. In fact, they are too consumed with their own lives, which include issues with their jobs, children, finances, etc. They have their own worries and fears, so they will not think twice about yours.

If you remind yourself of this truth, you will free yourself from your constraints. You will finally be able to take the necessary steps to reach your own goals and live your life the way you have always wanted to.

## Do not hesitate to question your thoughts.

Every time negative thoughts come into your mind, you have to question them. You have to ask yourself if you have to take the negative thought seriously. You will find yourself answering with a 'no'; because really, why would you take such thoughts seriously?

Then, you have to analyze the situation. Why did you come up with the negative thought? Perhaps, during that time, you were hungry or tired from working. These factors greatly contributed to the occurrence of your negative thoughts. Your mind may have also been clouded after having a bad day or making a minor mistake. Such experiences may have caused you to focus on the negative rather than the positive side of your life.

When you question your negative thoughts, you make yourself grounded. You become levelheaded and you gain a more sensible perspective. You realize that experiencing negativity does not erase the fact that positivity still exists.

**Replace negativity with positivity**.

Look around you and notice your surroundings. What do you see? What do you allow inside your mind? Whatever your answer is, it has a huge effect on your life. Thus, you have to be mindful of the thoughts that you allow inside your mind.

You have to question yourself regarding the top three negativity sources you have. The answer may pertain to people, music, social media, etc. Then, you have to question yourself about what you can do to lessen the amount of time you spend on these negativity sources.

Make it a point to follow up on this. Spend less time on your negativity sources and more time on your positivity sources.

**Refrain from turning molehills into mountains.**

In order for you to prevent negative thoughts from growing inside your mind, you have to confront them as soon as possible. You can also zoom them out by asking yourself if your current problems are still going to matter several weeks, months, or years from now. You are most likely going to figure out that your negative thoughts are not even going to matter in the future. Thus, you have to refrain from turning such molehills of negativity into mountains of negativity.

## Release your negative thoughts and talk about them.

Sometimes, letting things out and talking them over is the best solution for a problem. If you keep your negative thoughts inside your mind, there is a chance that they would grow. Hence, you have to release them. You can let them out and then talk about them with a friend or a therapist. Venting about the issues you have within you can help you unload the burden that you feel. It can also help you change your perspective about your situation and encourage you to search for feasible solutions or course of actions.

## Live your life and then come back to the moment.

If you find yourself starting to harbor negative thoughts, you might be recalling a past event or anticipating a future one. Your moods can be confusing and your thoughts troubling.

In order for you to get rid of such thoughts, you have to focus fully on the present moment. You have to be mindful of whatever is happening to you right at that moment. When you focus on the present, you will be more open-minded and less likely to engage in negative thinking.

One way to encourage yourself to focus on your present moment is to focus on your breathing. You can pause for a minute or two and then take deep breaths. When you inhale, see to it that the air goes in through your nose and fills up your belly. When you exhale, see to it that the air goes out through your mouth. As you repeatedly inhale and exhale, you have to focus on the air going in and out of your body alone. You should not think of anything else during this time.

Another ideal way on how you can focus on your present moment is to observe your surroundings and focus on the things that you see. You can take a break for one to two minutes, get your thoughts out of your mind, and then concentrate on the things that you see around you. You can also focus on the passers-by, the birds, the warmth of the sun on your skin, the smell of the freshly baked bread, or even the traffic noise in the streets.

### *Go to the gym for a quick workout session.*

Exercise gives you endorphins, which are natural chemicals that can make you happier. So, whenever you feel down, you should make an effort to exercise. If you have a hectic schedule and you cannot afford half an hour for a workout, you can simply do ten to fifteen minutes. The important thing is that you did it. It does not matter how long you exercised, as long as you did. In addition, working out helps you distract yourself from your negative thoughts. It helps you attain focus and may even encourage you to harbor positive thoughts.

## Do not allow your negative thoughts to bring you down.

A lot of people make the mistake of letting their fears get the best of them. If you are one of these people, you may choose to run away from your issues instead of facing them. You may have the impulse to avoid your fears, but you have to understand that they can get worse if you do not deal with them properly.

One of the best ways to deal with a situation like this is to ask yourself about the worst possible case that can occur. If you think about it thoroughly, you will realize that the worst-case scenario is not that bad. You will also be prompted to take action and reduce the possibility of it actually occurring. When you do this, you will have clarity and you fear will be lessened.

**Aim to help other people achieve positivity in their lives.**

If you allow yourself to be stuck with your negative thinking patterns or adopt a victim mentality, you will not improve and grow as a person. Thus, you have to get out of your head. You also have to redirect your energy onto someone else by helping that person gain positivity. When you do this, you will feel better as well as become more optimistic.

You can help another person gain positivity in their life by being kind, listening to them, and saying good things about them. It is not really difficult to do this. However, you have to genuinely want to do it in order for it to be effective.

**Practice gratitude and be thankful for everything that you have.**

When you become grateful for the little things that you have, you become more appreciative of the bigger things that you receive. Practicing gratitude also enables you to open yourself up for more blessings. Oftentimes, people get so caught up in their day to day lives that they forget to appreciate the wonderful things they have around them.

So, upon waking up in the morning, you should notice the blessings that you have such as sunlight, water, food, air, etc. You tend to neglect these things because you are used to having them on a daily basis. Imagine your life without them and you would be surprised of how much you actually need them. So, you have to make it a habit to practice gratitude on a regular basis. When you become grateful for your blessings, you receive more.

Showing gratitude for basic necessities in your life may seem odd because you are so used to having them but it is little, easy changes like this that can drastically begin to create a much more optimistic mindset.

# Chapter 4:

# 10 Easy Habits of Positive People

We've now touched on the power Negative Thinking possesses, and the easy tips and patterns you can accommodate to help overcome negative thoughts. Now, we will see how easy it can be to introduce different habits that positive people have, and how it continues to benefit their goals and lifestyle.

People who possess positive traits do not wait for their lives to unfold according to how they wanted them to be. Instead, they strive to reach their goals so that they can have the lives that they have always wanted. If you want to be a positive person, you have to adopt the following habits that positive people generally have:

## 1. Expect your plans to work out.

People who are positive tend to have this mindset that their plans are going to work out no matter what. Things may not always be the way they expected and situations may turn sour, but they still do not give up the hope that their plans are going to work out.

These people do not allow their worries and fears to get the best of them. They do not allow negative thoughts to grow in their minds. Instead, they visualize that their goals and plans have already happened. During times of struggle, they remain strong and persistent into achieving their goals. They have trouble just like everyone else, but they always find a way to overcome their obstacles and provide a solution to their problems.

Obstacles will present themselves throughout many tasks you take in life, but they are only obstacles, the whole point of an obstacle is for progress to be halted, and without these halts, we would create no measure of success, things would just happen without any sense of endeavor. Expecting obstacles to arise is preparation for success, and something positive people will always maintain.


## 2. Don't dwell on failure.

Failure is inevitable. There will be no success if there was no failure. Even the most successful people in the world have experienced failure at some point in their lives. However, what differentiates successful people from non-successful people is their determination to get back up and continue going.

Positive people do not allow themselves to stay down on the ground. When they fall, they pick themselves up immediately and continue doing what they have to do. They do not allow the failures they experience to affect their life. Negative people tend to lean towards depression, discouragement, and negative thinking patterns.

If you find yourself failing constantly, you can take a break to analyze your strategies. Perhaps, you can do something differently so that you can get a different result. You can rest for a while, but you should not stop. This is what positive people do. They recognize the time when they need to slow down and recharge, but they never stop permanently.

## 3. Keep yourself busy.

People who are positive and successful do not become idle. They always want to do something productive and beneficial to themselves and to the society. They aim for things, to get things done and they actually make it happen, whether it is big scale or small scale. They display this trait in their personal and professional relationships.

If you want to be a positive person, you must strive to keep yourself busy. You must consistently find ways to improve yourself and your life in general. You must not let external factors, such as the opinions of other people, bring you down and cause you to become unproductive. You must also not allow negative people to influence you into becoming lazy, unproductive, and ineffective.

## 4. Be the change.

If you want to see change, you have to start within yourself. Positive people do not wait for the change to happen. Instead, they create this change. They do not blame other people or their environment for the way their life turned out to be. They are aware that they have the capability to change their lives according to what they truly want.

Positive people also do not rely on good luck and/or miracles. They search for ways that can make them attain the changes that they strive for. They do not sit around and wait. They take action. They do not merely think of what they want to happen. Instead, they think of what they want, they recognize it, and then they act gallantly towards it.

## 5. Let go of your past.

Positive people do not allow themselves to get stuck or become stagnant. They know that dwelling on the negativity and entertaining negative thoughts will not do them any good. They know that replaying past events over and over in their minds is merely a waste of valuable time and energy. They know that this kind of behavior will prevent them from living their lives fully.

Positive people know how to let go, and they let go of whatever hinders their growth and potential. They set themselves free from the past so that they can enjoy the present and prepare for the future. They fill their minds with great future possibilities instead of painful past memories. They also focus on the present moment so that they can detach from negative thoughts.

## 6. Create happiness.

Positive people do not wait for happiness. Instead, they choose to create it. They also focus on success, enjoyment, and joyful events. They search for results and do not allow themselves to be discouraged by circumstances and negative people. They aim to improve their lives as well as achieve more satisfaction and happiness.

Their positive attitude helps them maintain positive thoughts while repelling negative thoughts. The more positive their thoughts become, the more peaceful they feel and the happier they get.

## 7. Live in the now.

Positive people choose to live in their present. They neither get stuck in the past nor get too anxious about the future. They are aware that they are in the present, so that is where they live. For these people, their past remains in the past and their future is yet to come.

Positive people accept their past. They have memories and learning experiences. However, instead of being stuck in the past, they use it as a tool to make their present better. They do not pine for the days when things seemed better. They are grateful for the present, and they make new memories.

These people also make plans for their future, but they do not forget the fact that they have to do well in their present in order to execute such plans for the future. They refrain from thinking too much of what might happen. They are aware that nobody can really see what the future brings and that all they can do is be prepared for it. The happiness is always in the pursuit.

## 8. Be solution focused.

People who are successful and positive focus on coming up with solutions. If they cannot find one, they create one. They do not wait around for someone else to give it to them. They trust in their own abilities to come up with good and effective solutions. They do not get stuck with limitations, but rather become empowered by possibilities.

Positive people concentrate on the things that they can do instead of the things that they cannot do. In addition, they are aware that the perfect solution does not exist, but they remain confident that they will come up with a good and fitting solution.

## 9. You're not the victim.

People who are successful and positive also do not play victim. They do not blame circumstances for victimizing them. They are the opposite of negative individuals who lack self-confidence and engage in negative thoughts. These people allow others to pull their strings, making them ineffective and miserable.

Positive people know better, which is why they do not blame others. They know that blaming circumstances and situations is not going to get them anywhere. They are confident in their own abilities. This is why they are independent, confident, and happy. They are productive and effective. Their positive attitude repels negative thoughts that attempt to go inside their minds.

## 10. Take charge.

And, last but not least, Take Charge! Positive people take charge. They accept full responsibility for the actions that they take and for the way their lives turn out. They do not wait for the circumstances or situations to change, but rather take the appropriate course of action to change them.

Positive people are empowered individuals. While they seek support and help from others, they do not solely rely on them. They do not wait for other people to come and help them because they help themselves. They also limit their interactions with people who may be toxic for their wellbeing.

They are aware of their basic human rights. They have high respect for themselves, so they do not feel like they are the victims. They do not hold grudges because they keep their mindsets positive. They forgive because they know that it will make them become better.

Introducing these 10 easy habits into your everyday lifestyle will soon see huge changes in your abilities to stay focused, to stay positive and to find true happiness inside. Once you've read all the points, try writing them down, be it on a phone, a pad or even on your bathroom mirror with some lipstick.

Whichever way will be most successful for you to be reminded each day, and start implementing theses habits.

# Chapter 5:

# The Key to Success and Happiness

People mostly strive for happiness. This is the very reason why there are so many self-help books, videos, audio files, and articles out there. People are consciously looking for the solution to be happy. Likewise, they keep searching for the path towards success. They attend seminars and workshops so that they can learn the strategies on how to be successful.

However, what most of these people do not realize is the fact that everything starts with themselves. As cliché as that sounds, it is true. You have to start with you. You have to acknowledge that you are capable of being happy and successful. You have to realize the fact that you cannot find happiness elsewhere unless you are happy with your own self.

With regard to success, success has a variety of definitions. A person may consider himself successful if he has a large house, an expensive car, and lots of money. Another person may also consider himself successful if he has good health, friends and family who support him, and a peaceful life. For most people, however, success equates to happiness.

## Does Success Inspire Happiness?

If you ask this question, a lot of people are most likely going to answer with a 'yes'. It actually makes sense. When you are successful, you are happy. Whether you pertain to success as financial success or lifestyle success, you still become happy if you are satisfied with the results. So, yes, success can inspire happiness but only if you learn how to be content with what you have while striving to be better.

There is nothing wrong with wanting for improvement. In fact, striving for something better is good for you. It prevents you from being stuck or stagnant. It inspires you to do more and to gain more. However, this kind of attitude and mentality becomes bad when you become greedy or discontent. You see, you have to appreciate your accomplishments no matter how little they seem. You have to be grateful for what you achieve.

## Does Happiness Inspire Success?

Just like the question above, a lot of people are most likely going to answer with a 'yes'. Well, if you are happy, you become motivated and inspired. You feel empowered and your confidence levels soar. This causes you to take actions that are beneficial for your growth. You become empowered to do the things that you have always wanted to do, whether it is shifting careers, starting a business, etc.

When you are inspired to do something great, you start to feel that nothing can stop you, not even the obstacles that come your way. You become determined in pursuing your goals, no matter how long it takes or how rough your path is. When you are happy, you think of all the possibilities. Positive thoughts do inspire success because they open the doors to creativity, hope, and courage.

This is why employers seek to make their employees happy. They know that their employees can become more productive at work if they are happy and inspired. People who are sad and cynical tend to be less effective. They often refuse to think outside the box because they do not believe that new ideas can be better. They are afraid to get out of their comfort zones and to try innovative things.

On the other hand, happy people are bolder and more courageous. They have this positive energy inside them that pushes them to move forward. They are more willing to take risks because they believe that trying and failing is better than not trying at all. They also consider failures and mistakes as learning experiences rather than setbacks.

## How to Achieve Both

Happiness and success go hand in hand. If you maintain a positive way of thinking, you will find it easier to achieve both. The following are some of the ways you can do to make you happy and successful at the same time:

*Practice gratitude.*

You have heard about this before. When you are grateful for your blessings, you receive more. Each time you receive something wonderful, you become happy, which in turn inspires you to take actions that can make you successful. At the same time, when you accomplish a milestone that signifies success, you feel happy. The cycle goes on and on. Nevertheless, practicing gratitude is key to achieve both happiness and success.

*Stay focused.*

Do not allow yourself to be distracted by anything that is not helpful to your growth. However, you should also not beat yourself up in case you fall down. When this happens, you have to pick yourself back up and continue. When you are focused, you become productive and reliable. You accomplish what you set out to do. You maintain your credibility and other people admire you for it. Then again, it is not their admiration or praise that keeps you going, but rather the happiness that you feel when you have helped them.

*Manage your time wisely.*

The saying that time is gold is true. Time is something that you can never get back once it has passed. This is why you have to make the most of it. If you want to be happy, you should do things that you love and are passionate about. If you want to be successful, you should do something that your future self will thank you for.

Refrain from wasting your time being idle or engaging in addictive behavior. Do your best to fight against procrastination because procrastinating can only lead to more problems. When you procrastinate, you will not be able to accomplish your tasks and you will prevent yourself from achieving your goals. Doing nothing also invites negative thoughts into your mind.

*Set SMARTER goals.*

According to a study, only eight percent of individuals who set goals on the first day of the year are actually able to achieve them. This is because these people do not really think their goals thoroughly. Oftentimes, they set goals on impulse. If you really want to achieve your goals, you have to be realistic. Ideally, you have to set SMARTER goals so that you can attain them.

**S**pecific. **M**eaningful. **A**chievable. **R**elevant. **T**ime-based. **E**valuated. **R**e-Adjusted

Setting SMARTER goals practically means that you have to be specific with your goals and that such goals should be meaningful, achievable, relevant, and time based. You also have to evaluate your goals as well as re-adjust your approach until you finally succeed in achieving them.

*Have a good morning routine.*

Each day, upon waking up, you must go about your morning routine. This should be empowering and uplifting. Your morning routine should inspire you to go through your day and stay focused. Oftentimes, people have a hard time going through their day because they already set themselves up for negativity in the morning.

If you wake up in a bad mood, chances are you are going to spend the rest of your day in a bad mood. It is a recipe for disaster. For example, if you spilled coffee on your shirt, you will be more irritable when you face the heavy morning traffic. When you get to the office, you will get more stressed out when you face the paperwork that you have to deal with. You will be in a negative mood until nighttime comes.

If you want to be happy and successful, you must start your day with a smile. You must spend your morning emitting positive energies. You can meditate or say a little prayer. You can also recite positive affirmations as you look at yourself in the mirror. You can also practice gratitude and be grateful for everything that you have – air, water, electricity, food, money, home, family, friends, job, etc. When you realize that there are so many things you can be thankful for, you will be in a positive mood and the positive energy will stay with you throughout the day.


*Deal with your MITs.*

MIT stands for Most Important Task. What are the tasks that are urgent and what are the tasks that are important? You have to determine which one is which so that you can effectively spend time and energy on them. Important yet non-urgent tasks are found in the Quadrant Two of effective time management process.

Important tasks are the ones that help you grow in the long run. Accomplishing your most important tasks is crucial for your success and happiness. Although it is not easy to do all the things you have to do, especially under stressful situations, you still have to do them. Stick it out and soon, you will reap the fruits of your perseverance and diligence.

*Focus on your health and overall wellness.*

The saying that health is wealth is also true. Just think of it, would you rather have a lot of money or have perfect health? Sensible people would choose the latter. This is because money cannot buy good health and/or life. If you neglect your health because all you do is work, you will suffer in the end. Even if you can afford hospitalization and medication, you have to realize that prevention is still better than a cure.

If you want to be happy, you must never neglect your health. If you are in good health, you will be able to accomplish more things. You will be able to spend more time with the people you love and care about. You will be able to engage in activities that please you as well as do things that you are passionate about. You will also be able to influence others and be a positive role model for them. When you are in good shape, you will be able to do a lot of things that will make you happy and successful.

# Chapter 6:
# Putting Positive Thinking Into Practice

It is easy to talk about positive thinking, but it can be quite hard to apply. You can say that you will never harbor negative thoughts again, but when you find yourself in a stressful situation, you may start losing confidence and having negative self-talk. You may also harbor negative thoughts when you experience obstacles, make mistakes, encounter toxic people, or be in unfavorable circumstances.

Then again, if you are truly determined to put positive thinking into practice, all of these negativities will not be able to prevent you from doing so. Positive thinking takes practice. The more you do it, the better you get at it. If you continue practicing it, it will soon become a habit. I can't stress that last point enough. Practice makes positive, and positive makes perfect.

**Comparisons Between Negative and Positive Phrases**

At times, it becomes confusing to distinguish negative phrases from positive ones. This is especially true if you have been used to speaking negatively. A lot of people are actually inclined to having negative communication.

First of all, you have to be aware of negative self-talk. Keep in mind that the way you speak to yourself sets the tone to how you treat yourself. If you keep telling yourself that you are ugly, dumb, or incapable of doing things, your confidence level will get lower and you will not be able to achieve your goals. When you engage in negative self-talk, you sabotage yourself before you even try doing something.

For example, if you are in a beauty pageant and you see that all the other contestants are beautiful, you must not engage in negative self-talk. If you tell yourself that you are ugly and fat compared to the other ladies in the pageant, you will not feel confident enough to carry yourself. If you tell yourself that you will never win because you do not stand a chance against them, you will not be able to perform your best.

Likewise, if you are at a job interview and you keep telling yourself that you will not get hired, you will not be able to give good answers to the interviewer's questions. If your self-esteem is low, you will also not be able to walk around with confidence or sit down with ease. You will look and act nervous and you will seem incompetent. You see, you have already sabotaged yourself before you even gave yourself a chance to show what you got.

You may also want to rephrase your sentences when you talk to yourself. For example, when you make a mistake, you can tell yourself that it is a good learning experience instead of beating yourself up for it. You can say "I did not win the beauty pageant this year, but this gives me another chance to prepare for next year" instead of "I did not win because I am not as beautiful or as tall as the other candidates." You can also say "This divorce gives me the opportunity to be on my own and do the things that I am passionate about" instead of "This divorce makes me miserable because I have no one and nobody loves me."

Negative phrases are easier to turn into positive phrases when you look at the bright side of things. Even in the most difficult circumstances, positive people are still able to see the light. You just have to examine your situation from different angles. You also have to be rational and not get carried away by your current emotions. When you become logical, you will see that there are ways on how you can make things better.

When it comes to communicating with other people, you also have to be mindful of what you say and how you deliver it. You have to be extra careful when you are pressured or when your time is limited. Once your words are out, there is no way you can get them back. Therefore, you must not allow your impatience or temper to get the best of you and negatively affect your communication.

While it is true that you do not have control over the way other people perceive phrases and sentences, you can still have a significant contribution to it. For example, negative communication may occur when you ignore the feelings of other people, when you do not express your feelings properly, and when you do not show respect towards others.

On the other hand, positive communication may occur when you express your thoughts and feelings directly, you acknowledge the feelings of others, and you display a caring and respectful attitude towards others.

## "I've never done that before < It's an opportunity to learn something new"

There is another difference between positive people and negative people. Positive people have a welcoming attitude towards new ideas while negative people prefer to get stuck in their old ways. Positive people are willing to take risks if it means that they can improve themselves or be in a better position while negative people are afraid to get out of their comfort zones because they think that they cannot bounce back in case failure occurs.

So, if you refuse to try new ideas or do things that you have never done before because you are afraid of failing, then you are a negative person. On the other hand, if you always take every opportunity as something that can lead to growth, prosperity, and success, then you are a positive person. Negative people are cowards but positive people are courageous.

If you keep staying where you are, you will never move forward. You may even be tempted to go backwards because you are too anxious about the future. Your negative thoughts hinder you from taking chances and making mistakes, which are all crucial for growth and success. If you want to be happy and successful, you have to accept the fact that nothing is certain. However, you have a much better chance of improving if you are willing to take risks and have no problem using mistakes and failures as learning experiences.

**Practicing Positive Thinking Everyday**

Positive thinking can make you healthier, happier, and more productive. It can also help you influence others. To help you practice positive thinking on a daily basis, you must follow these guidelines:

*Guide your energy.*

What does that mean? It means that you have to have positive thoughts in order to have positive energies. Quantum physics states that the vibrations you send out are what you attract. So, if you have positive energy, positive things will come to you. You will receive more blessings and love into your life. You will be happier and more successful.

*Practice visualization.*

According to Buddha, you become what you think of. So, if you think of yourself as a happy and successful person, you will really become a happy and successful person. Conversely, if you see yourself as a sad, cynical person, you will really live a miserable life. Your mind is very powerful. You have to use your powers wisely.

In psychology, creative visualization is the practice of aiming to affect the external world through changes in expectations and thoughts. When you practice visualization, you are able to do things that you previously did not think you can accomplish.

*Be compassionate.*

According to the Dalai Lama, you have to be compassionate if you want other people to be happy. Likewise, you have to be compassionate if you want yourself to be happy.

Yes, it may be hard to remain positive and calm when you are facing so much failures and adversities. However, you must view these things as challenges that you can overcome rather than punishments or situations that you can never get out of.

You have to be compassionate towards yourself and other people so that you can better understand situations. Do not blame yourself and do not blame others. Without compassion, you will not obtain the awareness that will help you nurture yourself.

*Be resilient.*

Positive people are resilient. Just like everyone else, they also experience loss. They make mistakes, lose loved ones, lose property, fail in business, etc. They are just like you. However, they choose to stay resilient amidst crisis and chaos. They are able to adapt, accept, and practice gratitude.

# Chapter 7:

# Being Positive In Bad Situations

As you know, it is not easy to be positive if the situation is negative. It is normal for people to feel down. Sadness is a natural emotion. However, you should not be sad for too long. If you do, you will become depressed. Depression can be debilitating. It can hinder your growth, happiness, and success. Even worse, it can affect the people around you, especially your family and friends. It can also affect your professional life.

**How to Maintain Positive**

Having a positive attitude is the most ideal way to overcome negative situations. However, you need to be disciplined, focused, and determined to do this.

First, you have to learn how to control your responses. This is actually crucial to staying positive during negative circumstances. You have to take a deep breath to calm yourself. You can also start counting to calm your mind. When your mind is calm and clear, you can come up with a better response.

It is never a good idea to respond to anything if your emotion is negative. In fact, you have to practice the popular saying that if you cannot say anything nice, you should not say anything at all.

If you are in a negative situation and you are in a bad mood, you are likely to say something insulting, provoking, or negative. If you open your mouth and utter these words, the people around you will also feel negative. All of you will be negative, and this can result in a much worse situation.

Some people prefer to forget the negative situations that they have been in. However, if you are a smart person, you will use these negative experiences as learning opportunities. You should view the negative situations that you have been in as something that can be helpful to you in the future.

If something happened to you in the past and your reaction did not make things better, perhaps you can change the way you react in order to change the outcome in case a similar situation occurs in the future. Rather than be ashamed of yourself for having experienced such situation, you have to congratulate yourself for overcoming it and for having the initiative to use it as a learning opportunity.

People who are positive and successful also make mistakes. After all, nobody is perfect. However, these people have no qualms admitting when they are wrong. They do not pretend to be right all the time. When they make a mistake, they own it, apologize, and make up for it. They also learn from it and move on. They do not allow their past mistakes to affect their present and future. Rather than deny their shortcomings, they strive to improve themselves.

## Seeing the Bright Side

It is true that you cannot control every external factor, but you can always control the way you respond to it. How you think affects the way you act towards every situation.

If you are a novelist and a publishing company rejects your work, do you get discouraged and quit writing, or do you continue to look for another publisher who will publish your work? If your house is destroyed by the typhoon, do you sink in depression or do you pull yourself together and look for solutions? If your business goes bankrupt, do you give up on your dreams or do you try again?

Successful people also have downtimes, but as you know, they always rise above. They also feel stressed out and get heartbroken due to failures. You just do not notice that because they choose to focus on the positive and continue reaching for their goals. You do not see their sufferings because they do not wallow in them. All you see are their success because that is what they focus on growing.

So, how can you see the bright side if there seems no bright side? First of all, you have to acknowledge the fact that there is a bright side. There are two sides to everything – the positive and the negative. Believe it or not, even the worst case scenarios can have some good in them.

Say, you got divorced and you lost all your money. Your initial reaction may be to get devastated. You lost a partner and you have no means to support yourself. How can there be any good side to this? Well, you have to calm yourself first. Sit down, relax, and meditate. Calm yourself so that your mind will be clear. When you are ready to analyze your situation in a more logical perspective that is when the positive changes are going to happen.

You are divorced, and your bank account is empty. You still have good health, don't you? You have family and friends who support you. You can go to your parents and talk to your siblings. You can have drinks with friends. You have to remain grateful for those people who still have your back.

Then, you have to be open to the possibility of finding someone new. You can take your time to heal, but you should not give up on love. You may not feel that you can be in a relationship again, but you will if you desire it. Focus on yourself and the things that make you happy. Work out, pamper yourself, and indulge in your hobbies. Doing the things you love can increase your confidence.

So, you think that you have no money. You can get a job. You should muster courage and go apply for a job. It does not have to be a high paying position right away. You can start at the bottom. The important thing is that you get a job and you have a means to support yourself.

You can regain your confidence little by little. As the days pass by, you will get better and better. Eventually, you will be able to look back at your past with peace in your heart. You will no longer feel bitter or angry because you have chosen to treat your negative experiences as learning opportunities.

# Chapter 8:

# Creating a Positive Atmosphere

Positive people do not only maintain a positive mindset and attitude. They also create and maintain a positive atmosphere. They know that if their environment is pleasant and calming, it would be easier for them to relax and harbor positive thoughts.

So, how can you create a positive atmosphere?

You can start with cleaning up your house. To prevent yourself from feeling overwhelmed, you have to start with one room at a time. You can start with your bedroom, living room, or kitchen – whatever feels right for you. When you have a clean home, you can feel calmer and more comfortable.

On the other hand, if there is clutter everywhere, you can get stressed. You may get stressed out even further if you are not able to find the things you need because you do not know where they are. You can be in a foul mood instantly if you step on something that is not supposed to be on the floor. Having a messy home can lead to a messy mind.

Similarly, you should clean your workstation. Your desk should only contain the essentials. Clean up your drawers and organize your files. If you have a ton of paperwork on your desk, it would be difficult for you to deal with all of them. You have to be organized and systematic so that you can be more productive. You should throw out anything that is no longer serving you well or is cluttering up your space, such as old documents and receipts, food wrappers, paper cups, etc.

Do not forget to clean your phone and computer. You have to organize your files into folders so that you can access them more easily. Delete any files, messages, or contact information that you no longer use. Make it a point to read your emails and classify them accordingly. If you are organized at work, you will be more productive and effective.

You can also play some soothing music in the background. Good music can add to an already good atmosphere. If you like incenses or scented candles, you can also light them to set the mood. Just be careful and never forget to blow out the candles to avoid accidents. You can also use lighting fixtures to set the mood of the place and make it more relaxing.

All theses little, easily achievable tips can be very useful in creating a positive atmosphere, it is then up to you to maintain it. Keep up with theses little habits, let them become a way of life.

It is also down to you to create that same positive atmosphere when you are on the move, and socializing with friends and family. Whether you're the life of the party, or a quiet talker, having a positive atmosphere around will always attract more positive outcomes.

# **Conclusion**

Thank you again for downloading this book!

I hope this book was successful in aiding you to become more efficient in Positive Thinking. I hope it has taught you how to overcome your negative thoughts, and helps you in becoming consistent in seeing, and acting, more positively, and that it can help you become a more successful, and ultimately, happier person. The next step is to apply the lessons that you have learned from this book and start changing your life for the better.

Now, its all up to you, so go out there and live the life you want, and remember that happiness is always in the pursuit.

Finally, if you enjoyed this book, then I'd like to ask you for a favor, would you be kind enough to leave a review for this book on Amazon? It'd be greatly appreciated! And, hopefully, if this book has served its purpose, they'll be positive reviews!

Click here to leave a review for this book on Amazon!

Thank you and good luck!

22985888R00038

Printed in Great Britain
by Amazon